Easy
Intermediate

One-Two-Three!

Perfect for solo, duet, or trio playing

Christmas

Brass

Twenty-one special arrangements for one, two, or three brass players...
or for any other combination of instruments featured in the *1-2-3!* series

Arranged by James Power

CHESTER MUSIC
part of **WiseMusic**Group

EXCLUSIVELY DISTRIBUTED BY
Hal•LEONARD®

Order No. PM 2420164R
ISBN 978-0-7119-9385-3
This book © Copyright 2003 Chester Music.

Instruments featured on the cover provided by Macari's Musical Instruments, London.
Models provided by Truly Scrumptious and Norrie Carr.
Photography by George Taylor.
Cover design by Chloë Alexander.
Printed in the United States of America.

Contents

Deck The Hall

Traditional

O Come All Ye Faithful

Traditional

While Shepherds Watched Their Flocks

George Frideric Handel

God Rest Ye Merry, Gentlemen

Traditional

Hark! The Herald Angels Sing

Felix Mendelssohn

O Little Town Of Bethlehem

Lewis H. Redner

It Came Upon The Midnight Clear

Richard Storrs Willis

The First Nowell

Traditional

A

Moderato

B

C

Christmas Christmas
Music by James Power

Ding Dong! Merrily On High

Traditional

D.%. al Fine
Fine

We Wish You A Merry Christmas

Traditional

Joy To The World

Traditional

Merrily

Silent Night

Franz Gruber

Away In A Manger

James R. Murray

Good King Wenceslas

Traditional

Once In Royal David's City

Henry J. Gauntlett

We Three Kings

John H. Hopkins, Jr.

Jingle Bells

J.S. Pierpont

Angels, From The Realms Of Glory

Henry T. Smart

The Holly and The Ivy

Traditional

Merrily

The Coventry Carol

Traditional

SOLO PLUS

An outstanding collection expertly arranged for the beginning soloist, available for
Alto Saxophone, Clarinet, Flute, Trumpet, and Violin.

Easy-to-intermediate arrangements include piano accompaniment in print
and on the digitally recorded, playalong CD.

BOOK AND CD, 38 PAGES, $12.95 EACH

Boogie & Blues

An outstanding collection of classic boogie and blues
tunes expertly arranged for the beginning soloist.
Thirteen songs, including *Blue Prelude,*
Save Your Love For Me, and *This Masquerade.*

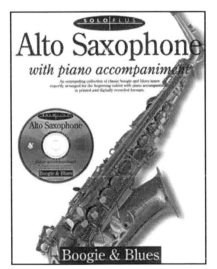

Solo Plus: Boogie & Blues:
Alto Saxophone
ISBN 0.8256.1673.5
UPC 7.52187.94737.0
AM947375

Solo Plus: Boogie & Blues: Clarinet
ISBN 0.8256.1671.9
UPC 7.52187.94735.6
AM947353

Solo Plus: Boogie & Blues: Flute
ISBN 0.8256.1672.7
UPC 7.52187.94736.3
AM947364

Solo Plus: Boogie & Blues: Trumpet
ISBN 0.8256.1674.3
UPC 7.52187.94738.7
AM947386

Solo Plus: Boogie & Blues: Violin
ISBN 0.8256.1762.6
UPC 7.52187.96139.0
AM961390

Christmas

An outstanding collection of fifteen classic Christmas tunes expertly arranged for the beginning soloist. Songs include *The First Noel, Jingle Bells, O Holy Night, Silent Night, What Child Is This*, and more favorites.

Solo Plus: Christmas: Alto Saxophone
ISBN 0.8256.1817.7
UPC 7.52187.96757.6
AM967571

Solo Plus: Christmas: Clarinet
ISBN 0.8256.1816.9
UPC 7.52187.96756.9
AM967560

Classical

Easy-to-intermediate arrangements of favorite tunes drawn from the folk and light classical repertories. Seventeen tunes, including: *To A Wild Rose, La Paloma, Rachmaninoff Piano Concerto No. 2*, and *Fantasie Impromptu*.

Solo Plus: Classical: Clarinet
ISBN 0.8256.1648.4
UPC 7.52187.94563.5
AM945637

Solo Plus: Classical: Flute
ISBN 0.8256.1649.2
UPC 7.52187.94564.2
AM945648

Solo Plus: Classical: Saxophone
ISBN 0.8256.1650.6
UPC 7.52187.94565.9
AM945659

Solo Plus: Classical: Trumpet
ISBN 0.8256.1651.4
UPC 7.52187.94566.6
AM945660

Solo Plus: Classical: Violin
ISBN 0.8256.1717.0
UPC 7.52187.94899.5
AM948992

Solo Plus: Christmas: Flute
ISBN 0.8256.1819.3
UPC 7.52187.96759.0
AM967593

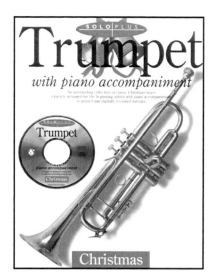

Solo Plus: Christmas: Trumpet
ISBN 0.8256.1818.5
UPC 7.52187.96758.3
AM967582

Solo Plus: Christmas: Violin
ISBN 0.8256.1820.7
UPC 7.52187.96760.6
AM967604

My First Recital

A superb collection of 23 light classics and folk songs from around the world, expertly arranged for the first-time recitalist. Songs include: *A Media Luz, Amaryllis, Matilda, Solace,* and *Trio.*

Solo Plus: My First Recital: Alto Saxophone
ISBN 0.8256.1682.4
UPC 7.52187.94745.5
AM947452

Solo Plus: My First Recital: Clarinet
ISBN 0.8256.1680.8
UPC 7.52187.94743.1
AM947430

Solo Plus: My First Recital: Flute
ISBN 0.8256.1681.6
UPC 7.52187.94744.8
AM947441

Solo Plus: My First Recital: Trumpet
ISBN 0.8256.1683.2
UPC 7.52187.94746.2
AM947463

Solo Plus: My First Recital: Violin
ISBN 0.8256.1656.5
UPC 7.52187.94571.0
AM945714

Standards & Jazz

Fourteen standards and jazz tunes, including *Angel Eyes, In Walked Bud, Darn That Dream, Imagination, Ladybird, Here's That Rainy Day, Like Someone In Love, Swinging On A Star,* and *Polka Dots* and *Moonbeams.*

Solo Plus: Standards & Jazz: Clarinet
ISBN 0.8256.1665.4
UPC 7.52187.94747.9
AM947474

Solo Plus: Standards & Jazz: Flute
ISBN 0.8256.1666.2
UPC 7.52187.94748.6
AM947485

Solo Plus: Standards & Jazz: Saxophone (Alto)
ISBN 0.8256.1667.0
UPC 7.52187.94749.3
AM947496

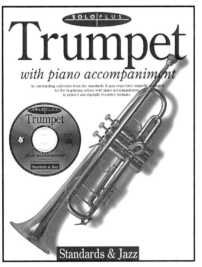

Solo Plus: Standards & Jazz: Trumpet
ISBN 0.8256.1668.9
UPC 7.52187.94750.9
AM947507

Solo Plus: Standards & Jazz: Violin
ISBN 0.8256.1719.7
UPC 7.52187.94900.8
AM949003